St. Peter's Fiesta

GLOUCESTER, MASSACHUSETTS

Written & Illustrated

by

Alice Gardner

www.alicegardnerstudio.com

Introduction

Do you know what a tradition is? It is something special people or a community enjoy doing year after year, usually at the same time and in the same place.

June 29th is the Feast Day of Saint Peter. To commemorate Saint Peter, it is a tradition in Gloucester, Massachusetts, to hold Saint Peter's Fiesta during the last weekend in June. Saint Peter, who was a fisherman, is believed to guard over and give special help to fishermen. Saint Peter, also known as Simon Peter, was one of Jesus' apostles. During Saint Peter's Fiesta, the people of Gloucester take the opportunity to thank Saint Peter for keeping the fishermen from the city safe during the year.

In 1927, sea captain Salvatore Favazza moved from Sicily, Italy, to the United States. Stories he heard of the seaside town of Gloucester reminded him of the home he left behind, so he decided to settle in Gloucester with his wife where they raised ten children.

Salvatore was so thankful for his blessings that he decided to have a statue built of Saint Peter. He chose a sculptor from Charlestown, Massachusetts.

Salvatore wanted to share the statue with his neighbors. He had the statue secured to a platform and eight strong fishermen carried it on their shoulders. Everyone in town joined the procession shouting, "Viva San Pietro! Ma che siamo tutti muti!"

The tradition of Saint Peter's Fiesta had begun and continues today.

To the people of
Gloucester of all ages:

Thank you for your
hospitality and wonderful sense
of community and tradition.

"Viva San Pietro!"
"Long live Saint Peter!"

"Ma che siamo tutti muti!"
"Are we all mute?"
or
"Shout louder!"

You know it is almost Saint Peter's Fiesta when . . .

you see the little sailor suits and dresses displayed in the window of the children's store downtown. The weather is getting warmer and school is almost out. Some say Saint Peter's Fiesta is better than Christmas!

Trucks and equipment arrive. Men begin to set up Saint Peter's altar . . .

and hang angels in the sky.

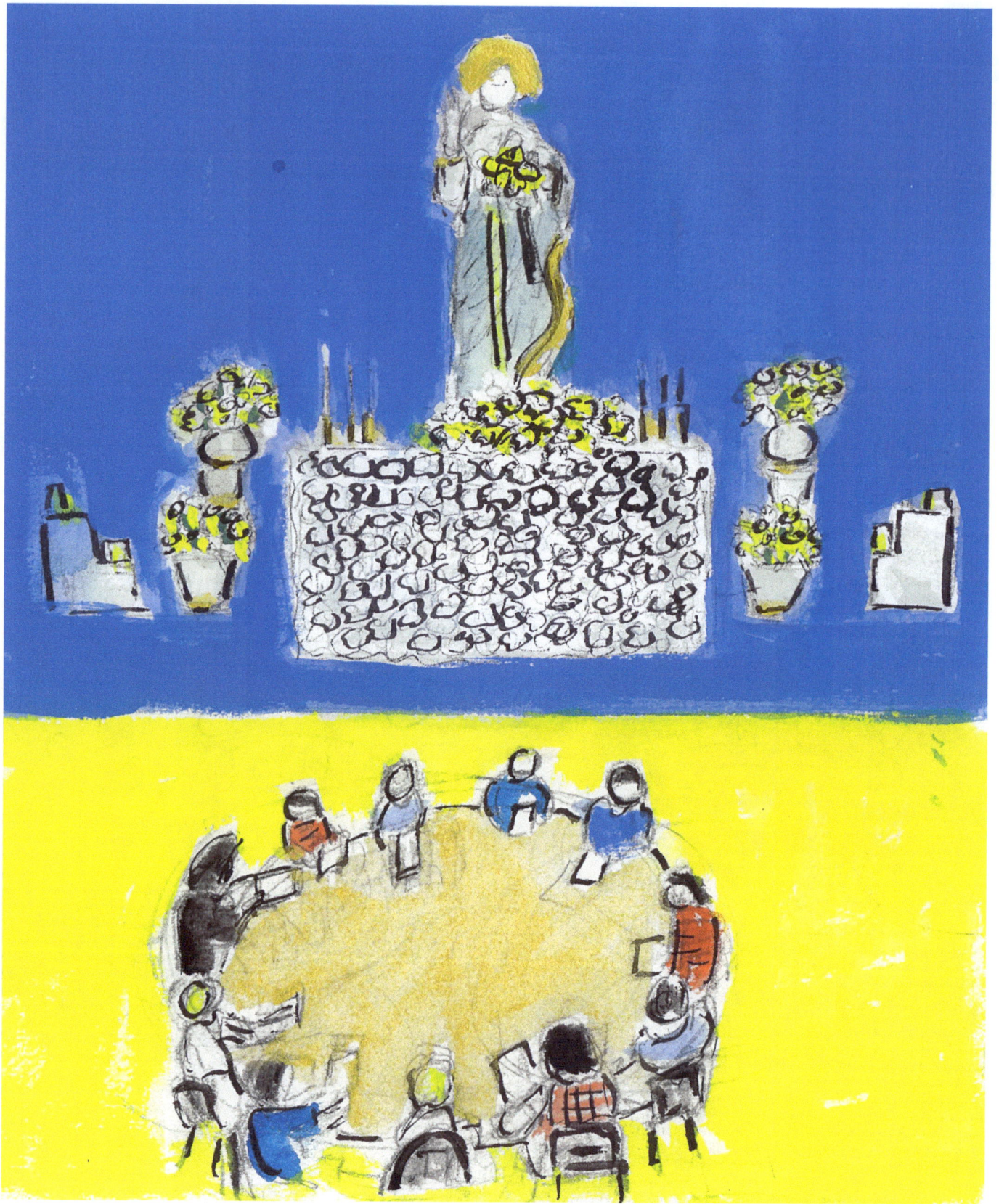

A novena, a series of special prayers, is held for nine evenings before the Fiesta. Women, men, and children gather at the American Legion Hall to sing prayers together in a Sicilian dialect they learned from their grandparents. They thank Saint Peter for keeping the fishermen safe.

A Ferris wheel appears in the sky. Food booths are set up.

Soon you can see the fishing boats arriving for Saint Peter's Fiesta. The Gloucester fishermen come home for seven days for the Fiesta.

It is a special time for them to see their families and friends, paint and repair their boats, decorate them for the Blessing of the Fleet, and take part in thanking Saint Peter for watching over them and keeping them safe.

DINNER:
ITALIAN SAUSAGE
CLAMS CASINO
EGGPLANT PARMESAN
STEAK MODIGA
BOLOGNESE PASTA
FRIED FISH
CALAMARI
BAKED STUFFED SHRIMP
MOZZARELLA AND
TOMATO SALAD

DESSERT:
"S" COOKIES
ALMOND MACAROONS
ITALIAN COOKIES
CANNOLIS
BROWNIES
LEMON GELATO

BEVERAGES:
WINE
ITALIAN SODA

Families in town are getting ready for the Fiesta by cooking many Italian dishes and desserts. Some families entertain as many as 350 people or more in their backyard on the Sunday of the Fiesta. They welcome aunts, uncles, cousins, grandparents, neighbors, friends, and the Greasy Pole walkers. Anyone who walks by is welcome!

"Sarai sempre il benvenuto qui!"
"You will always be welcome here!"

DESSERTS

FLORENTINES

ALMOND MACAROONS

RICOTTA LEMON

RAINBOW LAYER

BUTTER COOKIES

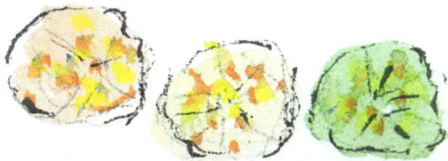

CASSATINI COOKIES

CANNOLI

CHAMPAGNE COOKIES

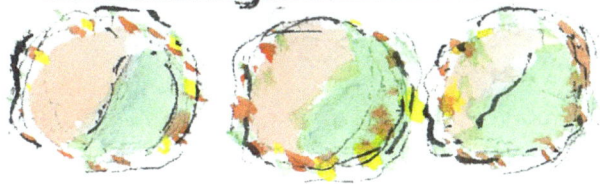

"S" Cookie Recipe

4 EGGS

1/2 CUP SOFT BUTTER OR 1/2 CUP CRISCO

1 CUP SUGAR

2 TEASPOONS GRATED LEMON RIND

1 TEASPOON LEMON EXTRACT

4 CUPS FLOUR

4 TEASPOONS BAKING POWDER

1. BEAT EGGS, BUTTER OR CRISCO, AND SUGAR TOGETHER
   UNTIL CREAMY.
2. MIX IN LEMON RIND AND LEMON EXTRACT.
3. GRADUALLY ADD THE FLOUR AND THE BAKING POWDER.
   BLEND WELL.
4. SHAPE INTO A LOG ON A FLOURED SURFACE.
5. CUT ONE SLICE AT A TIME AND ROLL INTO
   1/4–1/2-INCH "SNAKES."
6. FORM THE "SNAKE" INTO AN "S" SHAPE.
7. PUT ON COOKIE SHEETS LINED WITH PARCHMENT PAPER.
8. BAKE AT 375 DEGREES FOR ABOUT 10 MINUTES OR UNTIL
   LIGHTLY BROWNED.
9. LET COOL ON RACKS. FROST AND DECORATE WITH SPRINKLES.

FROSTING

1 TABLESPOON UNSALTED BUTTER

1/2 POUND SIFTED CONFECTIONER'S SUGAR

6 TABLESPOONS MILK

1. MELT BUTTER AND PUT IN A BOWL.
2. ADD CONFECTIONER'S SUGAR AND A LITTLE MILK AT A TIME
   UNTIL YOU HAVE THE DESIRED CONSISTENCY.

On Tuesday, the final day of the novena, many more people come and join in song and prayer. The local priest arrives and gives a message of hope and thanksgiving.

The official St. Peter's Fiesta pin for the year is given out to everyone. St. Peter's Fiesta has begun! Everyone shouts, "Viva San Pietro! Ma che siamo tutti muti!" Everyone is served delicious cassata cake and lemonade.

The statue of Saint Peter is taken off the stage, carried down the stairs, and attached to a platform. Eight fishermen carry him on their shoulders. Everyone follows the men and Saint Peter's statue to Beach Court where a Fiesta committee member is honored. The procession then returns to Saint Peter's Club where Saint Peter's statue is returned to the front window.

The formal opening of Saint Peter's Fiesta is on Friday. Saint Peter's statue is taken from the front window of Saint Peter's Club, attached to a platform, and carried on the fishermen's shoulders. Everyone lights a candle and walks with Saint Peter up the street, then they walk to Saint Peter's Square where Saint Peter's statue will be placed in the central part of the altar.

"Viva San Pietro! Ma che siamo tutti muti!"

Everyone sings "God Bless America" and waves little American flags. Children toss colorful confetti. A band plays and the mayor greets the people. "Welcome to Saint Peter's Fiesta. VIVA!"

St. Peter's Fiesta Children's Games

Saturday: Pie Eating and Watermelon Eating
Contest and Egg Toss
Beach Court – 3PM
Sunday: Pinata Breaking Contest
Pascucci Court – 6:30 PM

On Saturday, children gather on Beach Court for the Children's Games: the pie-eating contest, the watermelon-eating contest, and the egg-throwing contest. Watch out for the egg shells and egg yolks in the street!

Late in the day on Sunday, you can try to break the piñata at Pascucci Court.
When it breaks, there is more candy than you can imagine!

All weekend you can go to the carnival and ride the Ferris wheel, the merry-go-round, the Arctic Blast, and many other rides. You can try your luck at the duck game or throw a dart at a balloon and win a prize!

You can enjoy delicious fried dough with powdered sugar, cotton candy, and candy apples. Don't forget to try Ambie's famous sausages!

At ten o'clock on Sunday morning, families gather at Saint Peter's Square for the outdoor Celebration of Mass of Saint Peter. The Cardinal from Boston and local priests process in with the altar boys and girls. The choir sings "Lord, You Have Come to the Seashore." The cardinal talks about Saint Peter being a fisherman, he honors the Gloucester fishermen, he prays for their safety and prosperity, and he offers good wishes to the community.

Soon after the Mass, Saint Peter's procession begins.

The men who carry Saint Peter's statue stop as many as thirty times along the two-mile parade route. Each time they stop, they turn the statue toward a family who has lost a family member at sea, or has had a difficulty such as illness, to honor them. It is the hope that a special blessing will be bestowed on them from Saint Peter. The men also stop at Mother of Grace Club, Saint Ann Church, and Our Lady of Good Voyage Church where the statue of Saint Peter is blessed.

Children ride on floats which are all decorated with white tissue-paper flowers. They often dress as angels, saints, or fishermen.

Bands play! Drums roll! Everyone shouts, "Viva, viva, viva San Pietro! Ma che siamo tutti muti!"

Remembering Our Heritage
THE FORT
Bringing Back A Tradition
CARRYING OF THE OARS
"VIVA SAN PIETRO!"

At three o'clock on Sunday, people gather at Stacy Boulevard near the Fisherman's Memorial Statue for the Blessing of the Fleet. The Cardinal blesses the fishing boats which have gathered there and remembers boats of long ago. The people pray to keep the fishermen safe and for a good fishing year.

Next are the Seine Boat Races at Pavilion Beach. Each boat must row out one-half mile, turn around the flag, and row back. The first boat back to the beach is the winner. The first-place boat receives an American flag and the second-place boat receives an Italian flag.

The Nina, the Pinta, and the Santa Maria are the Seine boats in Saint Peter's Fiesta. They are manned by twelve crew members: ten rowers, a helmsman who steers, and a coxswain who makes sure all the rowers stay together.

The Greasy Pole walkers, dressed in colorful costumes, arrive at Pavilion Beach and are taken by boat to the Greasy Pole platform.

The Greasy Pole walkers must walk the 45-foot Greasy Pole protruding from a platform, 200 yards from shore, without falling in the ocean.

During the first round, called the "courtesy round," everyone gets a chance to walk the pole but they are not allowed to capture the flag. After that, the first walker to capture the flag is declared the winner.

The winner is carried on the shoulders of his fellow walkers and is paraded around town. Everyone shouts, "Viva, viva, viva San Pietro! Ma che siamo tutti muti!"

When night falls, bands play and people dance. The night is magical with sparkling lights and angels in the sky. At eleven o'clock, the men take Saint Peter's statue from the altar. You can follow the Saint Peter's procession around the Fort neighborhood.

Along the route, some people throw confetti from the windows of their homes. You can see the glow of the fireworks in the distance and the golden lights from the boats in the harbor.

As the procession reaches Saint Peter's Square, the lights of the Ferris wheel and the angels sparkle in the sky. Everyone follows Saint Peter's statue to Saint Peter's Club. There Saint Peter is carefully taken off the platform and carried inside. Everyone is shouting, "Viva San Pietro. Viva! Viva! Viva!"

The statue of Saint Peter is placed in the window. The statue will remain there until Saint Peter's Fiesta comes again next year. Everyone begins to sing "God Bless America."

The fishermen say goodbye to their families and go back out to sea.

"Goodbye, goodbye! We will miss you!"

Saint Peter's Fiesta is over until next year. But when you begin to see the sailor suits and dresses appear in the children's store downtown, when you see the men arrive to set up the altar, when you see the sparkling Ferris wheel and the angels in the sky, when the weather gets warmer and school is almost out, you know the tradition of Saint Peter's Fiesta is coming again to Gloucester, Massachusetts— passed down from one generation to the next.

Viva!

Did you know these fun facts about Saint Peter's Fiesta?

The Saint Peter's Fiesta committee meets all year long to work on every detail of the Fiesta.

It is a tradition for very young children to wear sailor suits and dresses to special events at the Fiesta. Everyone else wears white dresses, pants, and shirts.

Saint Peter's statue stands five feet tall. It weighs 600 pounds and the platform to carry it weighs 100 pounds! The eight men that carry it must be very strong!

You can buy a rose, or pin a dollar bill to the ribbons cascading from Saint Peter's statue, to contribute to Saint Peter's Fiesta fund.

The "Fort" neighborhood is located on a little peninsula of land jutting out over Gloucester Harbor. There was an actual fort there made of earth to protect the harbor during the Revolutionary War. The area is home to many Gloucester families. Most of Saint Peter's Fiesta activities are held "Down the Fort."

Traditional Fiesta Food!

Secret recipes are passed down from generation to generation.

There are three secrets to Sicilian cooking.
1) always listen to your Nona (Grandma) and Mom—they know best!
2) use the freshest ingredients possible
3) cook with family

It is a tradition for children to make "S" cookies and brownies for Saint Peter's Fiesta.

The traditional cassata cake for Saint Peter's Fiesta is a yellow sponge cake layered with vanilla pudding, chocolate pudding, and nuts. The cake is frosted with whipped cream and decorated with candied cherries. Yum!

Procession on Sunday

Saint Peter leads the procession, but there are seven other patron saints represented in the procession: Mother of Grace, Our Lady of Fatima, Saint Maria Annunciation, Maria Del Luma, Saint Maria Socconso, Our Lady of Aprecida, and Padre Pio.

Children, and often adults, carry oars with the names and colors of fishing boats to pay tribute to past and present fishing boats and fishermen. There can be up to 100 oars carried in the procession. Many people who have moved return to Gloucester every year to carry an oar to honor their family's fishing boat.

When the procession finally arrives back at Saint Peter's Club, everyone celebrates with showers of red, green, and white confetti.

Seine Boat Races

Seine boats were used long ago by fishermen to haul fish that were caught in floating nets. They set out from a larger boat, hauled in the fish, then returned to the mother boat.

Preliminary Seine races are held on Saturday. The top two winners race against the defending champion. There are also races for women and children on Friday.

Greasy Pole

The Greasy Pole originated in Sicily in the early 19th century or earlier. It was brought to Gloucester by Sicilian fishermen.

The first Greasy Pole contest took place in 1931 and was won by Nat Misuraca. Salvo Benson holds the all-time record with 11 wins. Peter Frontiero won seven straight Sunday contests from 1987–1993.

The grease on the pole is biodegradable axel grease which is sometimes mixed with banana peels, fruit cocktail, or Tabasco sauce to make it more slippery.

The Greasy Pole is five feet to the water's surface at high tide. At low tide, it is about 15–20 feet to the water. Rain can make the pole more slippery, while wind can throw walkers off balance; if it is a hot, sunny day, the grease turns to hot slime. The ocean temperature is about 60 degrees.

The winner can keep the captured flag as an award and his name is engraved on the Greasy Pole trophy.

I hope you love Saint Peter's Fiesta as much as I do. See you in June!

Acknowledgements

I would like to thank the following people for their invaluable help, encouragement, and suggestions during the creation of this book: Gloucester, Massachusetts, Mayor Sefatia Romeo Theken; Joe Novello and Anthony Cusumano, President and Treasurer of Saint Peter's Fiesta; Sara Favazza, daughter of the late Salvatore Favazza, founder of Saint Peter's Fiesta; Joey Ciaramitaro of *Good Morning Gloucester*; Rosalie Verga, head of the novena for Saint Peter's Fiesta; Maria D'Amico Cracchiolo, owner of Café Sicilia; Chris Orlando, owner of Kids Unlimited; Felicia Ciaramitaro Mohan, author of *Gifts of Gold* cookbook; Patricia Hodges, daughter of the late Leonardo Taormina, captain of the fishing trawler Taormina B pictured at the end of the book; Allison Varga, owner of the Pleasant Street Tea Company; and Janice Severance, Arwen Severance, and Abby Libro of The Bookstore of Gloucester.

Special thanks to Mary Sue Wonson, my writing buddy for many years and infinite source of encouragement and wisdom; Lorraine Cooper, Carol McKenna, Dean Donnelly, and Annamarie Lavieri who always believed in me; Sally Grimes who saved the *Gloucester Daily Times* articles about the Fiesta for me for over ten years; to my grandchildren Nate and Anna for their modeling expertise; and my husband David who helped edit and was never hesitant to offer suggestions.

Thank you to the *Gloucester Daily Times* for their wonderful coverage of Saint Peter's Fiesta over the years, especially the article about the Greasy Pole walkers called "Stand by Their Men" by Dan Guttenplan, filled with interesting facts about the Greasy Pole. Thank you as well to *Saint Peter's Fiesta, Through the Years*, a book compiled by The Young Men's Coalition. And thank you to the Cape Ann Reads program which inspired me to complete this book.

Many thanks and gratitude to my editor, Damaris Curran Herlihy, and to my designer, Cathy Kelley, for their fine work and wonderful enthusiasm and encouragement that helped make this book come together.

About the Author and Illustrator

Alice Gardner was inspired to write and illustrate
Saint Peter's Fiesta after attending the Fiesta for
the first time in 2000. She loved the joy, fun, and
color of every event, as well as its spirituality,
traditions, and wonderful sense of community.
She took many pictures, collected newspaper
articles, and painted many paintings of the Fiesta.
With the 90th anniversary of Saint Peter's Fiesta
on the horizon in 2017, she decided it was time
to create this picture book and dedicate it to the
people of Gloucester.

www.ingramcontent.com/pod-product-compliance
Lightning Source LLC
Chambersburg PA
CBHW061138030426
42334CB00004B/91